Endangered Animals of SOUTH AMERICA

Marie Allgor

PowerKiDS press™

New York

Published in 2011 by The Rosen Publishing Group, Inc.
29 East 21st Street, New York, NY 10010

First Edition

Editor: Jennifer Way
Book Design: Julio Gil

Photo Credits: Cover Dorling Kindersley/Getty Images; pp. 4, 5 (main, inset), 7, 11, 15 (main), 16–17, 17 (inset), 22 iStockphoto/Thinkstock; pp. 6, 15 (inset) Hemera/Thinkstock; p. 8 James P. Blair/Getty Images; p. 9 Joe McDonald/Getty Images; pp. 10, 14, 20 Shutterstock.com; p. 12 Joel Sartore/Getty Images; p. 13 Pete Oxford/Getty Images; p. 18 Thomas Marent/Visuals Unlimited, Inc./Getty Images; p. 19 Aldo Brando/Getty Images; p. 21 Picturegarden/Getty Images.

Library of Congress Cataloging-in-Publication Data

Allgor, Marie.
 Endangered animals of South America / by Marie Allgor. — 1st ed.
    p. cm. — (Save earth's animals!)
 Includes index.
 ISBN 978-1-4488-2533-2 (library binding) — ISBN 978-1-4488-2650-6 (pbk.) —
 ISBN 978-1-4488-2651-3 (6-pack)
 1. Endangered species—South America—Juvenile literature. 2. Wildlife conservation—South America—Juvenile literature. I. Title.
 QL84.3.A1A45 2011
 591.68098—dc22
                                     2010025757

Manufactured in the United States of America

CPSIA Compliance Information: Batch #WW11PK: For Further Information contact Rosen Publishing, New York, New York at 1-800-237-9932

Contents

Welcome to South America!

South America is the fourth-largest **continent** on Earth. Made up of 12 countries, it is bordered by the Pacific Ocean in the west and the Atlantic Ocean to the east. North America and the Caribbean Sea lie to its north.

Many different plant and animal **species** live in South America. However, more than 370 million people live in South America, too.

Llamas live in the Andes, in South America. These llamas are near Macchu Pichu, in Peru.

4

South America is home to many large cities, such as Rio de Janeiro, in Brazil. As cities grow, the natural habitats around them are destroyed.

Many places in South America have tropical rain forest climates. The rain forest shown here is around Iguazú Falls, which lies on the border between Argentina and Brazil.

These people need roads and places to live and work. They find the land and natural resources they need in the same places where many of these animals live. Because of this, many of South America's animals are **endangered**.

South America's Climate

South America has many different **climate zones**. More than half of South America has a tropical climate, which is warm and wet year-round. South America has hot, dry places, too. The hottest place in South America is in Argentina. It once reached 120° F (49° C) there. The wettest place on the continent is Colombia, which gets as much as 350 inches (889 cm) of rain each year.

The Humboldt penguin lives on rocky coasts and on islands off Peru and Chile. The number of these penguins has been dropping quickly mostly due to habitat loss.

The southern tip of South America has a cold climate. There are even glaciers, which are large pieces of ice.

South America has cold weather on its high mountaintops and at its southern tip. It also has places that are temperate, or not too hot or too cold.

Habitats in South America

South America has many different types of **habitats**, in which many different plants and animals live. For example vicuñas, spectacled bears, and Andean iguanas live in the mountain habitat of the Andes.

South America is home to the world's largest rain forest, the Amazon. Some of the animals there are caimans, anacondas, jaguars, birds, and monkeys.

Large parts of South America's rain forests have been cleared to make way for roads and farms. This is often done by cutting down the trees and then burning them.

This is a dwarf caiman. Caimans are crocodile-like reptiles that live near fast-flowing rivers and streams in South American forests.

It might sound like South America's animals have plenty of places to live. However, people are destroying South America's natural habitats every day. For example, 20 percent of the Amazon rain forest has been destroyed in the past 40 years. More is cut down or burned every year.

South America's Endangered Animals

South America is a beautiful place with many rich habitats. However, many of its animals are endangered. The animals on these pages are endangered and could one day become **extinct**.

MAP KEY

Three-Toed Sloth

Hyacinth Macaw

Golden Lion Tamarin

Scalloped Hammerhead Shark

Golden Poison Dart Frog

Brazilian Three-Banded Armadillo

Scalloped Hammerhead Shark

1. Brazilian Three-Banded Armadillo

As its name tells you, the Brazilian three-banded armadillo lives in Brazil. Over the past 10 to 12 years, its numbers have dropped by more than one-third.

2. Golden Poison Dart Frog

The golden poison dart frog lives in only one small part of Colombia. The poison that coats its skin makes it one of the most poisonous frogs on Earth.

3. Golden Lion Tamarin

The golden lion tamarin lives in a small river basin in Rio de Janeiro, Brazil. It was once listed as **critically** endangered. After 30 years of work, it is still endangered but doing much better.

4. Scalloped Hammerhead Shark

Scalloped hammerhead sharks are endangered worldwide. In South America, these sharks live near the coasts of Brazil, Costa Rica, and the Galápagos Islands.

5. Hyacinth Macaw

Hyacinth macaws are found in parts of Brazil, Bolivia, and Paraguay. There are between 4,000 and 7,500 of these birds left in their natural habitat.

6. Three-Toed Sloth

Three-toed sloths are one of the world's slowest mammals. These animals are in trouble due to habitat loss.

Where Endangered Animals Live

VENEZUELA
GUYANA
SURINAME
FRENCH GUIANA
COLOMBIA
ECUADOR
BRAZIL
PERU
BOLIVIA
PARAGUAY
CHILE
URUGUAY
ARGENTINA

South America

Brazilian Three-Banded Armadillo

The Brazilian three-banded armadillo is not like other armadillos. It does not dig burrows, as other armadillos do. It also has a special skill that most armadillos do not have. When in danger, it rolls itself into an **armored** ball.

This special skill makes it very easy for people to catch it. It was hunted so heavily that the species almost disappeared.

The Brazilian three-banded armadillo is threatened by more than just hunting. It is also endangered due to habitat loss.

In fact, it was believed to be extinct for many years. Luckily, a small number of these animals were found in the early 1990s. This species is in trouble due to habitat loss and to people who hunt the animal for meat.

Golden Lion Tamarin

In the 1960s, the golden lion tamarin was listed as critically endangered. In 1992, there were only about 272 of these monkeys living in their natural habitat in Brazil's rain forests. **Conservation** groups worked together to start **captive breeding** programs to help these tamarins. There are now more than 1,000 golden lion tamarins in the wild. They are still endangered, though.

The golden lion tamarin gets its name from its reddish orange fur, which looks like a lion's mane. A tamarin is a kind of monkey.

Hawks are another golden lion tamarin predator.

The golden lion tamarin is endangered mostly due to habitat destruction. Because so much of Brazil's rain forests have been cut down, tamarins live in small groups far away from each other. This makes it hard for tamarins to find other groups so that they can make babies.

Hyacinth Macaw

Hyacinth macaws are a kind of parrot. They are named for their beautiful blue color. These macaws live in open woodlands and palm swamps in Brazil. They do not generally live in the thicker parts of rain forests. They eat fruits, seeds, and some small animals.

It is unlawful to take hyacinth macaws from the wild today. However, there is still a lot of illegal trapping of them.

Hyacinth macaws are endangered mostly because of the pet trade. This means people catch these birds to be sold as pets. People also hunt them for their meat and their feathers. They are also in danger because their habitat is being taken over or destroyed by people to make land for animals or farms.

Golden Poison Dart Frog

Poison dart frogs are tiny frogs that live in the rain forests of Central and South America. They are known for their bright colors and for the poison in their skin. Many of these small frogs are endangered, including the golden poison dart frog.

The golden poison dart frog is a golden yellow frog. The poison in its skin is so strong that one frog has enough poison to

A fully grown golden poison dart frog is only about 2 inches (5 cm) long!

People have cut down forests throughout the golden poison dart frog's habitat.

kill 10 people! This frog is endangered because people have destroyed its habitat for logging and farms. They have also used **pesticides** on their crops, which have killed many of these frogs.

Three-Toed Sloth

Sloths are slow-moving animals that live in the rain forests of Central and South America. They hang from branches using their long claws and strong arms. They spend most of their time in trees, and most of that time is spent sleeping. They sleep for up to 20 hours a day! They eat leaves and fruit from the branches where they hang.

People hunt sloths for food and for sport. They are also hunted by animals such as jaguars.

Sloths are sometimes run over by cars on roads that go through rain forests. These slow-moving animals cannot get out of the way of cars.

There are six species of sloths in the world. Two species are two-toed sloths, and four species are three-toed sloths. Two species of the three-toed sloths are endangered because their forest homes are being cut down.

Save South America's Animals!

South America is an important place for **biodiversity** on Earth. Yet people are destroying it. People have been cutting down forests, dirtying or damming rivers, and changing the land of South America. Luckily, people have begun to understand how important the habitats in South America are. Lands have been set aside that are just for plants and animals.

Captive breeding programs help put animals back into their natural homes. Much still needs to be done. Every day more species become endangered. We must save South America's animals!

ARMORED (AR-merd) Having a hard shell that keeps something safe.

BIODIVERSITY (by-oh-dih-VER-sih-tee) The number of different types of living things in a place.

CAPTIVE BREEDING (KAP-tiv BREED-ing) Bringing animals together to have babies in a zoo or an aquarium instead of in the wild.

CLIMATE ZONES (KLY-mut ZOHNZ) Large places that have the same kind of weather.

CONSERVATION (kon-sur-VAY-shun) Keeping something safe.

CONTINENT (KON-tuh-nent) One of Earth's seven large landmasses.

CRITICALLY (KRIH-tih-kuh-lee) Being at a turning point.

ENDANGERED (in-DAYN-jerd) Describing an animal whose species or group has almost all died out.

EXTINCT (ik-STINGKT) No longer existing.

HABITATS (HA-buh-tats) The kinds of land where animals or plants naturally live.

PESTICIDES (PES-tuh-sydz) Poisons used to kill pests.

SPECIES (SPEE-sheez) One kind of living thing. All people are one species.

Index

B
biodiversity, 22

C
Caribbean Sea, 4
climate zones, 6
Colombia, 6, 10
conservation
  groups, 14
continent, 4, 6
countries, 4

D
danger, 12, 17

L
land, 5, 17, 22

M
mountaintops, 7

N
natural resources,
  5
North America, 4

P
Pacific Ocean, 4
pesticides, 19

plants, 8, 22

R
rain, 6
roads, 5

S
species, 4, 12–13,
  21–22

V
vicuñas, 8

Web Sites

Due to the changing nature of Internet links, PowerKids Press has developed an online list of Web sites related to the subject of this book. This site is updated regularly. Please use this link to access the list: www.powerkidslinks.com/sea/soamer/

31901051141143